Crescendo Publishing Presents

Instant Insights on...

EMPOWERMENT

MOTIVATION!
Your Master Key to Success & Riches

Parviz Firouzgar

small guides. BIG IMPACT.

Insights On...

MOTIVATION! Your Master Key to Success & Riches!
By Parviz Firouzgar

ISBN: 978-1-944177-35-5 (p)
ISBN: 978-1-944177-36-2 (e)

Crescendo Publishing, LLC
300 Carlsbad Village Drive
Ste. 108A, #443
Carlsbad, California 92008-2999

www.CrescendoPublishing.com
GetPublished@CrescendoPublishing.com

What You'll Learn in this Book

Most people find it very difficult to tap into their source of real motivation, and this keeps them from accomplishing anything that would provide real success and fulfillment in their lives. Instead, they lead a life of mediocrity, never knowing that they could easily break out and live their dreams by simply learning how to become motivated. There are specific reasons why people are not sufficiently motivated. There are also specific steps one can take to change that. It all begins with an understanding of where motivation comes from and how we can tap into it. There's more to it than meets the eye, but once we know, the rest becomes relatively simple.

In this book, you'll get **Instant Insights** on...

- Why motivational seminars rarely work because of something they all fail to tell you.

- Three different sources of motivation and the power each of them wields.

- How to get and stay motivated from the deepest core of your being.

- How to use this unstoppable source of motivation to your advantage so that making your dreams come true becomes a predetermined certainty.

A Gift from the Author

To help you implement the strategies mentioned in this *Instant Insights™* book and get the most value from the content, the author has prepared the following bonus gifts we know you will love:

A SECRET bonus chapter

You can get instant access to these complimentary materials here:
www.parvizfirouzgar.com.

Table of Contents

Dedication

I dedicate this book to my son Gabriel.
May you discover your core desires and live a
purpose-driven life.

Introduction

Motivation is defined as the reason or reasons one has for acting or behaving in a particular way. Motivation is used to explain the cause of our behavior. It represents the reasons for our actions, desires, and needs.

This definition of motivation should surprise few people. We all use the word frequently, typically in its correct context. The concept of what motivates us is part of our daily conversation and our commonly accepted belief system. But the reality is that there's a lot more to motivation than meets the eye. The purpose of this book is to provide you with transformational insights into the topic of motivation that can change your life for the better.

Why is motivation so all-encompassing important? It is because motivation provides us with a single-minded purpose and this is the starting point for all individual achievement. The reason for this is in the results that having purpose, inspired by being motivated, provides us, including self-discipline, determination, courage, energy and effort, enthusiasm and creativity, and a 'failure is not an option' attitude.

Few people understand the different types of motivation, where each comes from, and the effect they have on us. Even less is known about how powerful the right kind of motivation can be versus the kind we typically deal with, thinking that's all there is. The right kind of motivation holds powers that few of us can even imagine. But again, it has to be the right kind of motivation as there are several types. One has to know how to tap into it if one wants to harness its unbelievable potential to move mountains and make happen what most of us would define as impossible.

The problem is that although we talk about motivation regularly, most people are actually not very motivated. Part of the reason is that most people have never learned where true motivation comes from and therefore don't tap into this fountain of creativity and action. Another problem that results from this lack of knowledge is the poor decisions we make throughout our lives because we are not properly motivated. This leads to an unfulfilled life where we are not living our true purpose or doing that which we are passionate about.

This book aims to solve many of these issues by showing what different types of motivation there are, where they come from, and how we can tap into them to realize any goal or dream we may have. Once you know how to get and stay motivated in a way you've never experienced before, nothing can stand in your way to accomplish that which may seem totally out of reach to you now. In fact, that which seems difficult will become easy, and that which seems impossible will become merely difficult.

The Problem

Why is it that most people are not very motivated? It is because they don't do what needs to be done to become and stay truly motivated — because they don't know how. Without motivation there is very little we can accomplish. Sure, our boss may threaten us with termination if we don't do as he asks. This type of negative motivation, as in avoiding getting fired, may mobilize us to temporarily be somewhat productive at work, but that type of motivation occupies the lowest rung on the ladder of motivation. It is also the arena within which most of us operate for most of our lives.

In my opinion the only place where negative motivation finds a worthwhile home is in marketing. Sometimes we buy something to avoid a negative outcome if we don't have that particular product or service, and that's okay as long as this marketing technique is responsibly used.

As we learn to move up the ladder from negative to positive motivation, we move into entirely new territory where fulfilling our dreams becomes the outcome, not just avoiding a negative result.

Even those individuals who seek motivation by spending thousands of dollars on motivational seminars typically don't stay motivated for very long. In fact, have you ever met someone who went to a motivational seminar, such as a multiday Tony Robbins event, and then came home pumped up with so much motivation that they could barely contain their excitement? Not only that, they genuinely learned so much valuable information that they knew they were now fully prepared to put their lives on a trajectory of never-ending growth and success.

When you see them, their excitement and enthusiasm are so radiant that you and other people around them become convinced of the value of the education and motivation they just received. And you are right: they did receive powerful information and motivation on how to become successful. But then the strangest thing happens. Just a few weeks later their life ends up exactly where it started before the seminar: no change, no growth, no excitement, and no more ambition. WHAT JUST HAPPENED?

Here's what the vast majority of personal-growth and motivational seminars, books, audio programs, and coaches fail to tell you: This type of motivation is like food and water. You cannot eat and drink just one day and expect not to need to do it again the next day. Likewise, you cannot go to the gym for just a week and expect the gains to last. It is the same with motivation. We must feed ourselves motivational material on virtually a daily basis for the material to have a lasting impact on our lives. Motivation can come to us from books, audio recordings we may listen to as we drive our cars, or seminars we may occasionally attend. This is why even the most impactful, profound seminars rarely have a lasting effect. The motivational boost simply wears off after a few weeks — or sooner.

This lesson was recently emphasized for me in a way I will never forget. I saw Bob Proctor, a personal-growth guru, give a one-and-a-half-hour long speech at an entrepreneurial seminar called CEO Space. At eighty-two years old, he did not use any notes and offered his audience a wealth of information. He was amazing to observe. One small story he told made the entire session valuable beyond words. He said that even after a lifetime of being absorbed in the personal-growth world, he still reads a bit of Napoleon Hill's *Think and Grow Rich* every single day! Wow. This hit home. It confirmed the validity of what I am telling you. You *must* consume personal-growth material on an ongoing basis for the rest of your life if you want to continue to grow and reach ever higher levels of success. It is the only way. If Bob Proctor still does it, then we definitely need to also.

Fortunately there is a beneficial bonus or side effect to becoming absorbed in personal-growth material: a dramatic boost in your happiness. The reason is that you will soon feel more in control of your future, and the mental boost this gives you is worth the effort. The increase in your happiness can be quite substantial, and it alone will make your absorption into the world of personal growth worthwhile.

Always remember that motivation needs to be an ongoing process. Why most personal-growth trainers don't tell you this vitally important fact is beyond me, but hopefully you will heed my advice. In order to stay motivated and reap the resulting benefits, you must become absorbed in motivational or personal-growth material on a daily basis.

Your Instant Insights...

- Most people are not very motivated.

- The majority of people live a life where their only motivation is negative; that is, avoiding an undesired outcome such as getting fired. This is the lowest form of motivation.

- To remain positively motivated, we must consume motivational material on a daily basis.

External Motivation

There are three major types of positive motivation, and each comes from a different source. As I describe each in its own chapter, they move from least powerful to the final one, which is so powerful that it can be considered one of the greatest forces in the universe. Tap into it and you become unstoppable. In fact, as you'll see, it requires several chapters to detail every aspect of it.

Let's start with the most common source of motivation. Although it is the least powerful, its force still has the potential to transform lives from the mundane to happiness, success, and fulfillment. It can even make you wealthy beyond your wildest dreams.

Motivation that comes from outside influences is the first type and comes mostly from reading material, audio programs, seminars, or coaches. Despite the fact that it is external, it can still have a profound impact on our lives — but only if it is repeated and added to continuously, that is, daily.

External motivation does not come from within us. It is therefore superficial and can have a lasting impact only if repeated regularly. Here is an example to illustrate my point.

Having been a student of personal-growth material my entire adult life, its effects on my success in life and business have been obvious. For this reason many people come to me for counsel when they are faced with a problem, whether it's personal or business related. As much as I enjoy giving the best advice I can, the outcome has also been a source of endless frustration for me.

For example, a typical scenario is an hour-long conversation over the phone or in person designed to give the individual I am counseling the guidance he or she needs to get unstuck and moving in the right direction. Since I typically know what I'm talking about, the effect my advice has on the other party becomes quickly obvious. I have frequently been told, "Oh my, you are so right! That is exactly what I need to do. You've really motivated me to take action. Now I know what to do. Thank you so much!" I then observe them over the next few weeks, and to my utter dismay, sometimes absolutely nothing happens. Some people never even take the first step toward solving their dilemma.

For many years I could not figure out why my advice did not have the desired effect when the other party openly acknowledged that my advice was spot-on and their intention was to immediately follow it. It was a source of deep frustration for me — until I figured out what was going on. Any kind of advice, in whatever form it is delivered — words, books, or whatever — is advice that comes from the outside. It is external. For external motivation to have a real and lasting impact, it must be repeated regularly or the effect quickly fades. Nobody tells you this, and nobody told me either. I had to figure it out on my own. When I did, it was a revelation.

Internal motivation, the type that comes from within us, is entirely different because it does not have to be repeated in the same way; it is already a part of us. The real challenge with internal motivation is recognizing it; that is, finding out what motivates us. It is not always obvious, and it is different for every person.

Internal motivation comes in two forms, passion and core desires. Both are addressed separately in the next few chapters.

"One of the strange facts concerning men who move with definiteness of purpose is the readiness with which the world steps aside so that they may pass, even coming to their aid in carrying out their aims."

– Napoleon Hill

Your Instant Insights...

- External motivation is a motivating force that comes from outside us, such as from books, audio recordings, seminars, or a coaching session.

- External motivation must be repeated regularly for it to have any lasting impact.

- For external motivation to become a lasting part of us, we must immerse ourselves in it until it is integrated into our being. Even then, however, we must never stop feeding ourselves with the message.

Internal Motivation – Passion

The second-most powerful source of motivation is internal, and it is being passionate about something. At the very least it should be something in which we are very interested. Although passion originates inside us, interests can be developed and turned into passions; that is, an external interest can be internalized to become a passion that now motivates from within. Once internalized, it is there to stay.

Being passionate about what you do in life is one of the foundational requirements to becoming successful. The importance of this cannot be overemphasized. There are specific reasons for why passion is an absolute requirement for success.

Becoming successful requires work — sometimes long, hard work. When you are passionate about your life's work, you look forward to getting up and going to work each day. In fact, if you love what you do, it's not really work, is it?

Then, when we are passionate about what we do, we will let nothing stand in our way. Our mistakes and the obstacles we will inevitably encounter become mere roadblocks that are nothing but temporary setbacks and learning experiences. We do not give up, and failure is simply not an option. Our passion for something — and therefore our motivation to accomplish what we set out to do — will never go away. It cannot be extinguished if it is genuine. This is the power of passion.

I have always taken this concept to the extreme. That is, almost every business I have ever started was one that I knew nothing about. However, I was extremely interested in that type of business with the potential to become passionate about it. In retrospect I can see that the power of my passion has never failed me. Most of my businesses became multimillion-dollar enterprises after just a year or two, even though I knew nothing about the industry initially.

There is one other benefit to the power of passion that will contribute to your success. To succeed at something we have to become an expert at it. Passion enables us to learn what we have to learn in record time. Have you ever tried to read a page of something you are just not interested in? It is nearly impossible as you reread the same passage over and over again, yet it still won't sink in. But when you are deeply interested in the subject, you cannot get enough of it, and learning becomes a breeze.

Passion gives our activities meaning, which leads to fulfillment, which is my definition of success. Success is doing what you love and making a good living doing it. That's fulfillment. The money will automatically follow and should never be the primary motivating factor. We all know rich people who are miserable as can be as they are not doing something they love. In fact, their becoming rich was probably a fluke in the first place, if not the result of outright unethical behavior. We'll discuss this in more detail later.

If you do what you are passionate about, success becomes almost a certainty, and if riches are something you also want to acquire, that process is not difficult once you are living your dream. With the right knowledge, any activity can be turned into an economic powerhouse. But the chances of becoming wealthy purely for the sake of becoming monetarily wealthy are slim to none.

Anyone can tap into the power of passion. It comes from the outside by finding something in which we are deeply interested, and then it is internalized as it converts into a passion that becomes an immensely powerful motivational force.

"Temporary defeat is but a testing ground which may prove a blessing in disguise if not accepted as final."

– Napoleon Hill

Your Instant Insights...

- Passion provides us with the energy and motivation to do what is necessary.

- Being interested in or passionate about something gives us the ability to learn everything we need to become an expert in our field.

- Interest in an external source of motivation that is internalized when it becomes our passion. Then it is there to stay.

Internal Motivation – Core Desires

The final and most powerful source of motivation comes from our core values and core desires. Each of us has core values that define who we are and what we believe in. They cannot be altered as they permeate every fiber of our being.

A core desire is akin to an obsessive burning desire, one we cannot forget or let go of even if we tried. We are willing to pay any price for its attainment. Procrastination disappears as our obsession leads us unwaveringly toward the realization of our goal where we will not allow anything to stand in our way.

Think about core values or core desires like this: Imagine a couple that decides to get married, but one thing they fail to discuss beforehand is whether or not they both want children. As it turns out, she passionately wants a large family, but he does not. These are core desires, and there can be no compromise. The unfortunate result in this situation is almost inevitably divorce. What this means is that both will eventually fulfill their core desires, just not with each other. The forces that these core desires generate in our lives are so strong that if we don't follow them, extreme unhappiness and lack of fulfillment result. We must follow our core desires. Even if we try to fight them, eventually they will overcome us, and more often than not, we will simply have no choice in the matter.

For this reason, every couple should share their core desires and discuss whether they are compatible with each other. They have to be for a relationship to work and thrive in the long run. The discussion should even move into less profound territory, such as what makes one feel loved. Even this can be a make-it or break-it compatibility issue. Here is a story to illustrate my point.

Imagine a couple who start out in a blissfully happy, fulfilling relationship. He tells her many times a day how much he loves her and he appears to be all she ever dreamed of in a man. Then one day the relationship starts to feel less solid. He senses a bit of distance from her, but he still loves her like before and tells her this daily.

He does everything he can think of to make her happy, yet over time it becomes obvious that she is beginning to drift farther and farther away.

As the situation deteriorates, he becomes increasingly frustrated as he has no idea what he is doing wrong or what is causing her to move away from him emotionally. Finally, the situation gets to a point where he cannot stay silent anymore; he asks her what happened. They were so happy together, yet now she clearly does not reciprocate his love in the same way she used to.

When he asks her why she is being so distant, she responds, "I don't feel loved."

"You don't feel loved?" he replies. "How can that be? You know how much I love you. I tell you many times each day that I love you, yet you are still moving away from me. It is killing me, and I don't know what is happening. I tell you constantly that I love you. How can you not feel loved?"

"I know you tell me every day — but you never buy me flowers anymore," she says sadly.

This story might seem a bit simplistic, but it is actually quite real. What makes us feel loved is a core value. It is who we are, and it cannot be changed. Some people need to hear "I love you" regularly while others feel loved through physical contact. Some may feel it from little gifts, such as flowers as in our story. Whatever the case may be, core values cannot be ignored, compromised, or replaced. We must pay attention to our core values in order for our lives to have meaning — or in this case for a relationship to work.

The major revelation is the amazing power our core desires and values hold. Personal-growth author, speaker, and coach Jack Zufelt refers to the power that our core desires wield as the conquering force. Zufelt has built an entire career around this one aspect of the personal-growth industry. To use his terminology, the conquering force that comes from our core desires is essentially one of the most powerful forces known to man.

Linking our core desires to inspiration as well as motivation also helps define them and illustrate their power. The word "inspiration" comes from the Latin word *inspirare*, which means "inspirit" or "divine guidance." When you are inspired to do something, you feel that you are being called to act. You don't have to do anything further to motivate yourself. Once you are inspired, action becomes effortless, and rather than procrastinating, you experience the opposite — a pull toward immediate action. Your passion doesn't diminish or extinguish. Inspired people feel aligned with their purpose, and as such it becomes obvious that their motivation comes from deep within.

Some people believe that motivation is only about pushing yourself to do something whereas inspiration is a sense of being pulled to do something, a driving force. This ignores the fact that there are three different types of motivation, external and internal forces, each with a different level of motivational power. They consider only weak motivational forces like doing something we should do but really don't want to do. In reality, inspiration is essentially the same as internal motivation, the strongest type of motivation.

Core desires can be almost anything: serving others, teaching, creating, excelling at sports, or anything that motivates a person from the deepest core of their being. Core desires go beyond mere passion as passion is something that can be developed. We can develop an interest in something, which in turn may become a passion that we enjoy immensely. In other words, it can be developed. A core desire, on the other hand, is a deeper part of who we are. It is already there and probably always was and always will be. But despite its permanent nature, the majority of people do not know what their core desires are. Some may think they know, but as we shall see, most do not. Fortunately, there are ways of finding out what our core desires are — which is our next topic.

"If you have your heart fixed on what you want there is nothing I can do to stop you from getting it."

– Andrew Carnegie's response to Charles M. Schwab after being asked for a promotion

Your Instant Insights...

- Our core desires are our most powerful motivational force.
- Core desires cannot be ignored, changed, or replaced.
- Core desires originate from deep within us.

How to Find Your Core Desire

As previously mentioned, most of us do not know what our true core desires are and therefore have a really hard time trying to figure out what would truly motivate us from the deepest core of our being. Since that is where the power to accomplish practically anything lies, finding out what our core values and desires are is a vital exercise if we want to make success a predetermined certainty. It is also what we need to find out if we want to unleash the force within us that has the power to make dreams come true — dreams that may seem impossible today but that can become part of our reality tomorrow.

Many of us think we know what truly motivates us from deep within, but as you will see, many of us are not digging deep enough. We need to discover our deepest desires. What we think are our deepest desires are typically just paths or stepping-stones to our true core desires. If this concept seems vague or ambiguous to you, don't worry, I'll clear this up for you shortly and help you discover the highest motivating power within you.

Let's start with some exercises that will help you get to know yourself better. These will assist you in discovering who you really are and what motivates you from the deepest seat within your soul. The first is an exercise that was given to the audience at a seminar I attended many years ago. It helped me immediately discover what motivates me from deep within, and it will help you also. The speaker said he would ask us a question and we had to write down the first word that came to mind. The question was, "Who are you?" Instantly the word "teacher" popped into my head, and I was totally surprised by this. That was not who I thought I was. Later, in retrospect, I realized that it was right on. I get an enormous sense of fulfillment when I can impart knowledge to another individual that then helps them solve a problem, become more successful, or better themselves in some way.

Years later I realized that the word "creator" also defines who I am. Most of the businesses I have built involved some sort of invention or new creation, whether it was a new product, a new service, or a new way of doing something that had never been done before in that way. Even writing this book is a combination of teaching and creating. I am creating the information in book format and teaching it to my readers. For this reason, with whatever venture I decide to pursue, I always make sure that those two ingredients are incorporated in it. It helps to guarantee that the venture will be successful because of all the motivation this unleashes within me.

So now ask yourself, "Who am I?" Write down the first word or words that come to mind. They can be very revealing when it comes to your core desires.

The next exercise is to ask yourself the following question: "If money were not an object, what would I be doing?" This question drills even deeper toward your core desires. It doesn't matter what your answer is; just write down what comes to mind. It does not have to be a business; it can be an activity you enjoy beyond anything else. Remember that whatever it is you enjoy most, that activity can either be turned into a business or it can be an ingredient in a business. For example, if there is nothing you enjoy doing more than reading, you could become a book editor for a publisher. If there's nothing you enjoy more than traveling, then becoming a tour guide or becoming a writer for a travel magazine could become your new vocation. The possibilities are endless for any kind of passion. You just have to use your creativity to determine the many different ways your passion can be a part of how you spend your time to make a living.

Our final exercise will get you directly to your deepest core desire. This exercise is best done with someone who understands the process because you may not know when your answer is just a stepping-stone to get to your true core desire. Effective as it may be to recognize this stepping-stone, discovering the core desire it leads to is vitally important if you want to tap into the full motivational potential of your core desire. Here's the exercise that will also illustrate what I mean. It is a matter of continuing to dig deeper until you get to the source, your deepest core desire.

Let's assume I asked you what your number one goal is in life. What is your dream, your passion? What would you like to be doing more than anything else? Ask yourself these questions, and write down your answer. It's okay to spend some time thinking about what it is you want to be doing more than anything else in life.

For the sake of illustrating this technique, let's assume that your answer is to become a successful investor in the stock market. Here's where the digging deeper part begins. My next question to you would be why do you want to become a successful investor? We then discover from you that the reason is so that you can become rich. Okay, but I'm going to continue digging even deeper because becoming a successful investor is obviously not your core desire since it leads to something else — becoming rich. I also don't think that becoming rich is your end-all and be-all. And it shouldn't be. So now I'm going to ask you why you want to become rich. Assume that your answer will be so that you can spend more time with your family.

Why do you want to spend more time with your family? "Because I love my spouse and children more than anything else in the world," you respond.

We just found your core desire! It is spending as much time as possible with what you love the most in the world, your family. Becoming a successful investor was not your core desire. Becoming rich was not your core desire. Being with your family is your core desire. One just led to the other. The technique is to simply keep asking why you want something until there is no new answer. In this case, spending time with your family does not lead to anything else you want. You just want that more than anything else.

This example illustrates the reason most of us don't know what our core desire is and hence what our greatest motivating force is. We think it's one thing, but the reality is we bring up something that just leads us to something else, and therefore closer to our real core desire. When you find it, then you've found what for you will be your strongest motivating force.

From the above example, if being with your family is your strongest motivating force, nothing will keep you from doing that. If it means you need to become rich so that you don't have to go to work, then there is nothing that will keep you from becoming rich so that you can essentially retire early and spend all your time with your spouse and raising your children. You will be motivated enough to overcome all obstacles to arrive at your goal. That level of motivation has the power to move mountains. The word "failure" will simply be eliminated from your vocabulary. Nonetheless, although your core desire is already within you, if you don't recognize it, you may never achieve it and therefore never achieve complete happiness and fulfillment. That's why you need to go through this exercise to discover your true core desire.

Also note that you may have more than one core desire. Discovering all of them, in addition to the answers you provided from the three exercises in this chapter, will allow you to get to know yourself in a much more meaningful way.

Your Instant Insights...

- Get to know who you are by simply asking yourself "Who am I?" See what word immediately comes to mind.

- Discover what you'd most like to spend your time on by eliminating the issue of money.

- Dig deeper and deeper by asking why you want something until you arrive at your true core desire. Repeat the exercise as you may have more than one core desire.

Money Motivation

After doing the exercises in the previous chapter, I know that some of my readers will conclude that their greatest motivation is money. One reason will be that you did not dig deep enough by really intensely contemplating why you want monetary wealth. The other reason is that you truly believe that money is your core desire. It is the latter group I want to address in this chapter.

There is nothing wrong with money. Money is a tool that should be used as a means to an end — but not as an end in itself. Whenever money is the end-all and be-all for someone, it often leads to very negative results, such as greed, corruption, cheating, self-serving materialism, and stepping on anyone to get more money. It becomes a never-ending quest for more money and power. I think we already have more than enough of that all around us. The relentless pursuit of more profit never benefits anyone. In the end it does not even benefit those who are receiving the profits.

Let's start by discussing the positive side of money, using it as a tool to do good. Some people know how to use it as a productive tool while others resent it, probably because they don't have any. Our population is divided into two halves. The first half are those who frown upon monetary wealth yet claim they care more about the ills in the world. These people are typically not wealthy and do not do anything to help their fellow man except to proclaim how much they care. It is symbolism over substance.

The other half of the population realizes that just caring isn't going to help anyone. If you want to help your fellow man, you need to have money to do so. This is one of the reasons they set out to become wealthy, so that they really can make a difference in the world, as many wealthy people do. Often they are also fulfilling a core desire in the process, that of helping people in need. Money becomes their means of achieving their core desire. These are the doers of the world, and they typically aren't worried about what other people think of them. They just want to do good for its own sake and don't always seek the admiration of others.

The symbolism over substance crowd is the opposite. They do not have the monetary ability to make a difference but demand admiration for how much they care. Draw your own conclusions, and also contemplate where you stand on this spectrum.

If you are still convinced that money is your primary core desire, then I urge you to continue digging deeper as true fulfillment cannot come from just being wealthy. We all know rich people who are miserable. In addition, however, and closer to most people's reality than the world of riches, studies have been done inside large corporations to see if salary levels contribute to job satisfaction. The results were that the level of one's salary has very little to do with overall job satisfaction.

If you still rank money at the top of your core desires, at the very least try to find another core desire within you that should then receive more attention than your desire for riches. You can still become wealthy in the process of pursuing a more worthwhile desire; just don't make wealth your primary focus. The road to riches that exists only for riches' sake is paved with problems.

It has been said that money will make a good man better and a bad man worse. There is a lot of truth to this statement. When money is the primary source of motivation, it will probably not be used for good purposes. If it is used for good, then money was never the primary motivator to begin with.

In summary, there is nothing wrong with wanting to become wealthy. It is one of the only ways we can help others in need. Money also contributes to paying for our health, our education, and a lifestyle that we may enjoy. But when it comes to our journey toward success, money should be a natural by-product, not our primary source of motivation. True fulfillment never comes from money alone. It comes from living your core desires, which more often than not, will and should involve serving others in some way.

"Money alone cannot make you happy but it does allow you to afford the kind of misery you enjoy the most."

– Author unknown

Your Instant Insights...

- Money is a tool that is neither good nor bad. It depends on how it is used.

- If you think money is your core desire, you may not be digging deep enough within yourself. Often it is just a path to achieve your true core desire.

- If you are convinced that monetary wealth is a core desire of yours then you should find another core desire to place more focus on. Allow wealth to be a byproduct on your road to fulfillment, not the primary focus.

Self-Discipline

A topic of utmost importance that must be addressed is self-discipline because self-discipline is possible only if we are properly motivated. Self-discipline is the one personality trait that the majority of us lack, making it impossible for us to move beyond our sea of mediocrity into the ocean of success and wealth.

Lack of self-discipline is so widespread and so deeply ingrained in us that it has become almost an epidemic. Unfortunately, we see it becoming worse with every generation as parenting skills have deteriorated into ineffective new-age experiments where disciplining our children is frowned upon. Undisciplined children will naturally become adults without any self-discipline. There is only one way to overcome this dilemma and that is to recognize the problem and then take matters into our own hands. The way to do it is via a massive self-imposed motivational force.

The topic of self-discipline is also widely misunderstood because most people don't understand how difficult it is to become self-disciplined. As mentioned, our generation is at a disadvantage, and most people don't even realize or acknowledge our own shortcomings in this respect.

To gain an understanding of the degree of the problem, an extreme but highly accurate analogy is to look at an individual who is addicted to a strong narcotic, such as cocaine or heroin. For that individual to successfully go "cold turkey" and overcome their addiction, they must have an overwhelming motivational force. The reward they receive when they become free of addiction must be greater than the force of the addiction itself. Very often we find that not even the potential of health or even survival is enough to overcome such an addiction.

Here's how this relates to all of us: We are all addicts. We may not be addicted to illegal narcotics, but we are all addicted to destructive habits such as procrastination, laziness, self-imposed limitations, fear of failure, conformity, or even the desire to be liked by everyone. These can be just as powerful as an addictive drug.

Here's where I'm going with all of this: The most destructive habit is not being in control of our thoughts, our internal environment, because controlling that environment is the number one required foundation of all achievement. The unnecessary and often damaging chatter that goes on in our minds from morning until night is probably the most detrimental addiction of all — and the hardest to break. It is also precisely where most people go astray on their road to success because learning to control our thoughts is one of the hardest forms of self-discipline known to man. Keep in mind that our internal environment (our thoughts) creates our external environment, not the other way around. So without this form of self-discipline, all other exercises that lead toward success are a waste of time.

Although this book is not about controlling our thoughts to create that which we want to manifest in the material world, know that numerous books have been written on just this one topic. Its importance cannot be underestimated or ignored. In fact, recognition of this vital ingredient is what created the modern personal-growth industry in the first place, most notably when Napoleon Hill wrote the most famous of all personal-growth books, *Think and Grow Rich.*

If the concept of creating your external world by controlling your thoughts and thinking the right kind of thoughts is new to you, then pick up one of the great books on the topic, such as *Think and Grow Rich*, *As Man Thinketh*, *As You Think So Shall You Become*, *The Secret*, and numerous others. More books have been written on this aspect of personal growth and success than any other.

Whichever habit it is that holds us back, breaking out of our habit is one of the hardest things we can do — unless we are motivated in such a way that the motivation provided is stronger than the habit we must break to move forward. For this reason we must be motivated by the strongest of all sources, our core desires, and preferably all three sources, to overcome this barrier. It takes powerful motivation to break our destructive habits, especially the habit of out-of-control thoughts.

To become successful we must abandon procrastination, laziness, and a host of other bad habits. Being motivated by a purpose-driven life is the solution, as it will provide us with the self-discipline we need. It is the only way.

"The mind that is properly disciplined and directed to definite ends is an irresistible power that recognizes no such reality as permanent defeat. It organizes defeat and converts it into victory; making stepping-stones of stumbling blocks; hitches its wagon to a star and uses the forces of the universe to carry it within easy grasp of its every desire."

– Napoleon Hill

Your Instant Insights...

- Lack of self-discipline is an epidemic.
- The most destructive habit is uncontrolled thoughts as it is our thoughts that create our external world.
- The only way to have enough self-discipline to learn to control our thoughts is through powerful motivation.

Combining All Three Sources of Motivation - What Can It Do for You?

Let's first discuss the ill effects that lack of motivation can have on our lives. First and foremost, it will mean that we are doing something we are not passionate about. Most nine-to-five employees are in this predicament. They live a life of mediocrity, wishing they could break out, but they don't know how. Therefore, they never do. The result is never feeling fulfilled and therefore never experiencing true happiness. Success will remain a concept that will apply only to a select few individuals without any prospect of us ever joining their ranks.

Making bad decisions as a result of not being properly motivated is a topic we have already touched upon. Here is another story to illustrate how this affects many of us. It will also illustrate some of the possible reasons for our self-destructive behavior.

I have a close friend who suffers from anxiety, and he has been on medication for quite some time. Granted, he does have some genuine issues in his life that make his anxiety understandable, and I feel deep sympathy for his plight. We recently discussed his situation because I wanted to find out exactly how he suffered. I do not have such panic attacks so it is a little hard for me to relate to what he is going through. Our discussion brought his suffering into clearer perspective for me.

Then, just a few days after our discussion, I happened upon a nutritional article discussing the epidemic of magnesium deficiency in our country and the maladies that this deficiency causes. One of them was anxiety. I immediately forwarded the article to my friend, hoping that maybe this finding could help him alleviate and possibly even cure his symptoms. I also found out that my friend was not taking magnesium supplements.

A week later I asked him if he started taking magnesium. The answer was no. Another week later I asked again. Same answer. One more week passed and he had still not taken this obvious step to potentially help his dilemma. I thought about the situation and, although deeply disappointed, realized that his lack of action was not uncommon. Even when you are offered exactly what you need on a silver platter and you need only to reach out and accept your gift, many simply will not. Why? Is it the "not invented here syndrome" where many people don't like to accept solutions unless they are of their own design? Possibly, but I think the underlying issue has to do with motivation. Because my friend lacked motivation at this stage in his life, even something as simple as trying a supplement to resolve his problem was out of reach for him.

We continued with more discussions, and I tried my best to help him find a goal and a purpose in his life to boost his morale. I believed it would alleviate much of his struggle. I was right. Once he found a new direction in life and something to look forward to, he suddenly started taking magnesium supplements. I'm not claiming that he suddenly discovered his core desire, but he did move up the ladder from unmotivated to somewhat motivated. And it clearly helped.

There is a lesson in this for all of us. Once we are motivated and begin to live a purpose-driven life, the benefits permeate all aspects of our lives. So let's continue to discuss the benefits of getting ourselves motivated.

Imagine you know what you are most passionate about, that which resides at the deepest core of your being. Imagine also that you know that the motivation that comes from knowing your core desires is a force that has the ability to fulfill, ***without any chance of failure***, those dreams that would make you live the life of greatness you were destined for. This is the promise of unleashing the greatest force known to man, the unstoppable power of a person who knows what he or she wants. You can have that power. It is the motivation that comes from deep, deep within. Better yet, when you allow yourself to be guided by motivational forces from all three sources we discussed, you will become absolutely unstoppable.

If you let yourself be motivated to the maximum extent possible from all three sources of motivation as described, you will live a purpose-driven life. The results are happiness, fulfillment, achievement, productivity, and most importantly no regrets. This is an important point. Numerous studies have been done asking people in the twilight of their lives what their greatest regrets are. Topping the list is almost always not taking enough risks in life and therefore not having lived their dreams. Those regrets become nonexistent for people who are driven by purpose. History is filled with achievers who followed their calling, from Leonardo da Vinci, Michelangelo, Benjamin Franklin, Henry Ford, and Nikola Tesla, to Albert

Einstein, Martin Luther King Jr., Mother Teresa, Ayn Rand, Bob Marley, and Steve Jobs, just to name a few. In the end they had no regrets. They did what they were born to do. And for this we will remember them forever.

You do not need to become world famous to live your purpose. There are millions of people who have lived a purpose-driven, fulfilled life without us ever having heard of them. But all of these people demonstrate the best of humanity. They have done good for others as well as for themselves. A legacy such as theirs is one we should all aspire to emulate, even if it doesn't make headlines.

Will you get yourself motivated so that you will spend your life doing what God and the universe intended for you? Will you immerse yourself in personal-growth information on a daily basis, follow your interests and your passions, and dig deep within yourself to discover your true core desire or desires? If yes, then prepare to live a life that others will look up to and remember. Give yourself the gift of true happiness and fulfillment. It is your purpose.

Your Instant Insights...

- Integrating all three sources of motivation will lead you to live a purpose-driven life.

- Not being motivated will cause you to engage in self-destructive behavior.

- Applying all three sources of motivation will make you unstoppable when it comes to achieving what you were born to do.

About the Author

For twenty-five years Parviz Firouzgar has been the owner of numerous multimillion-dollar companies, both for profit and nonprofit entities, in a variety of industries, sometimes running several ventures simultaneously. Some of Parviz's companies involved the use of investor funds of up to several million dollars. One investor walked away with a $1.7 million profit in just one year as a result of his confidence in the Parviz's abilities when he was just in his twenties.

Parviz founded a mortgage company and employed over 500 loan officers. He wrote business plans for start-up companies that helped them raise many millions in start-up capital. After he discovered a new way of raising funds, he expanded into the charitable arena. Within one year, his company was supporting 2,300 needy children around the world, providing all their food, clothing, and education.

Parviz has been in the direct mail and sweepstakes business, mailing so many millions of pieces of mail each month that his local post office had to expand their operations. Most recently, he has been in the precious metals and diamond business, including owning a gold mine.

Parviz was a radio talk-show host and a long-time instructor for Income Builders International (IBI), now called CEO Space, an entrepreneurial forum with internationally recognized instructors, such as Jack Canfield, Mark Victor Hansen, Bob Proctor, T. Harv Eker, John Gray, and Lisa Nichols.

Raised in Europe, Parviz speaks four languages. He has been accepted for membership in Mensa and Intertel, both high-IQ societies.

Connect with the Author

Website:
www.ParvizFirouzgar.com

Email:
Parviz@ParvizFirouzgar.com

Social Media:
Facebook: www.facebook.com/pfirouzgar

LinkedIn: www.linkedin.com/pub/parviz-firouzgar/b6/8b4/91

Twitter: @ParvizFirouzgar

Mailing Address:
13681 Newport Ave. #8-619, Tustin, CA 92780

Other Books by this Author

20/20 Hindsight
If I knew then what I know now, I'd be a whole lot richer!

20/20 Hindsight (Part II)
More lessons for entrepreneurs you won't learn about in business school!

The Secrets of Wealth
Discover the financial principles responsible for every fortune ever made and learn to use these principles to create your own fortune!

About Crescendo Publishing

Crescendo Publishing is a boutique-style, concierge VIP publishing company assisting entrepreneurs with writing, publishing, and promoting their books for the purposes of lead-generation and achieving global platform growth, then monetizing it for even more income opportunities.

Check out some of our latest best-selling AuthorPreneurs at http://CrescendoPublishing. com/new-authors/.

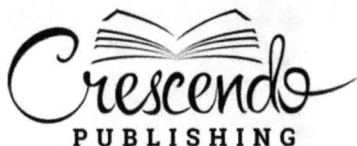

About the Instant Insights™ Book Series

The *Instant Insights™ Book Series* is a fact-only, short-read, book series written by EXPERTS in very specialized categories. These high-value, high-quality books can be produced in ONLY 6-8 weeks, from concept to launch, in BOTH PRINT & eBOOK Formats!

This book series is FOR YOU if:

- You are an expert in your niche or area of specialty

- You want to write a book to position yourself as an expert

- You want YOUR OWN book – NOT a chapter in someone else's book

- You want to have a book to give to people when you're speaking at events or simply networking

- You want to have it available quickly

- You don't have the time to invest in writing a 200-page full book

- You don't have a ton of money to invest in the production of a full book – editing, cover design, interior layout, best-seller promotion

- You don't have a ton of time to invest in finding quality contractors for the production of your book – editing, cover design, interior layout, best-seller promotion

For more information on how you can become an *Instant Insights™* author,
visit **www.InstantInsightsBooks.com**

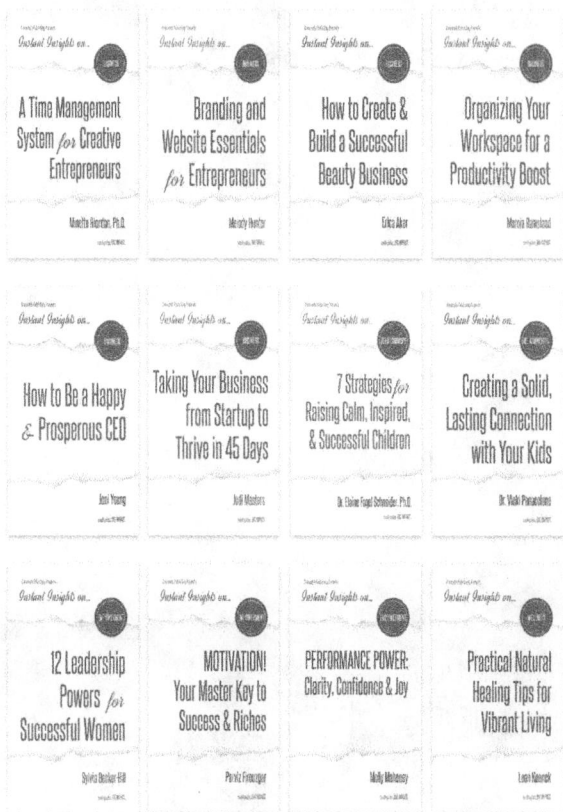

www.ingramcontent.com/pod-product-compliance
Lightning Source LLC
Chambersburg PA
CBHW060518280326
41933CB00014B/3015